COLUMBARIUM

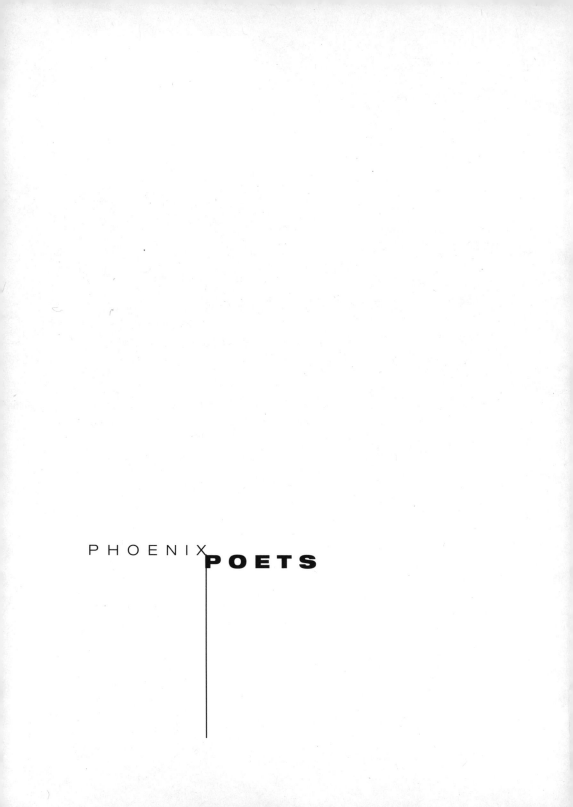

P H O E N I X **POETS**

COLUMBARIUM

SUSAN STEWART

THE UNIVERSITY OF CHICAGO PRESS
Chicago and London

The University of Chicago Press, Chicago 60637
The University of Chicago Press, Ltd., London
© 2003 by The University of Chicago
All rights reserved. Published 2003
Paperback edition 2005
Printed in the United States of America

12 11 10 09 08 07 06 05   3 4 5

ISBN: 0-226-77443-0 (cloth)
ISBN: 0-226-77444-9 (paperback)

Library of Congress Cataloging-in-Publication Data

Stewart, Susan (Susan A.), 1952–
      Columbarium / Susan Stewart.
            p.   cm. — (Phoenix poets)
      Includes bibliographical references.
ISBN 0-226-77443-0 (alk. paper)
      I. Title. II. Series.

PS3569.T474C65 2003
811'.54—dc21

                                        2003048354

columbarium —
a. *pigeon-house; dove-cote*
b. *a subterranean sepulcher, having in its walls niches or holes for*
    cinerary urns

— OXFORD ENGLISH DICTIONARY

Now let us make in each soul a sort of aviary of all kinds of birds; some in flocks separate from the others, some in small groups, and others flying about singly here and there among all the rest.

Then we must say that when we are children this receptacle is empty; and by the birds we must understand pieces of knowledge. When anyone takes possession of a piece of knowledge and shuts it up in the pen, we should say he has learned or has found out the thing of which this is the knowledge; and knowing, we should say, is this.

Now think: when he hunts again for any one of the pieces of knowledge that he chooses, and takes it and "has" it, then lets it go again, what words are appropriate here?

— PLATO, *Theaetetus*

Contents

III THE ELEMENTS

Acknowledgments

Grateful acknowledgment is made to the editors of publications in which these poems, or versions of them, first appeared:

American Poetry Review: "Bees," "Braid," "Dark the Star," "Ellipse," "Pear," "Rewind," "Scarecrow," "Weather," "Wings," and all of "Sung from the generation of AIR"

Critical Quarterly: "I had a little dove," as the final section of "Authentic Songs"

Electronic Poetry Review: "Forms of Forts" and "Unless and Until"

Free Verse: "Lost Rules of Usage," "Vigil," and "To You and For You"

The Kenyon Review: "Wrought from the generation of EARTH" and "The Rose" (New Series, summer/fall 2003, vol. 25, no. 3/4)

Ploughshares: "Shadow/ Lintel" and "Shadow/ Shadow" (vol. 25, no. 4)

Salt: "Drawn from the generation of FIRE," "Cross/X," "Shadow/Isaiah," "Jump," "Kingfisher Carol," "The History of Quiver," and "X/cross"

Stand: "Let me tell you about my marvelous god" and "The Seasons"

TriQuarterly: "Apple," "Night Songs," "Now in the Minute" (under the title "Awaken"), "Flown from the generation of WATER," "What You Said About the Moon," "Zero," "Lightning," and "These Trees in Particular"

X-Connect: "From 'Lessons from Television'" *Writers of the Information Age II,* CrossConnect, Inc., 1997

"Wings" was reprinted in *The Best American Poetry 2000,* edited by Rita Dove and David Lehman and in the *Jahrbuch der lyrik 2001,* edited by Christoph Buchwald and Adolf Endler. Munchen: Verlag C. H. Beck.

"Now in the minute," under the title "Awaken," was first issued as part of an edition of an art work by Ann Hamilton entitled, "Awaken." The work is a wool blanket hand-stitched with the poem in a bookbinder's box with accompanying printed text of the poem as well. New York: Mary Kelly; Cypher Editions, 2000.

"Apple" was reprinted in *The Best American Poetry 2001,* edited by Robert Hass and David Lehman.

"Let me tell you about my marvelous god" and "The Seasons" were reprinted with "Two Brief Views of Hell" in *Hammer and Blaze: A Gathering of Contemporary Poets,* ed. Ellen Bryant Voigt and Heather McHugh, 2002.

"Sung from the generation of AIR," "Drawn from the generation of FIRE," "Wrought from the generation of EARTH," and "Flown from the generation of WATER" were written for *The Elements,* an artist's book with lithographs by Enid Mark, published by ELM Press in 2002.

"O" was reprinted in Robert Harrison's *The Dominion of the Dead.* Chicago: University of Chicago Press, 2003.

*

My thanks to the MacArthur Foundation for a fellowship that helped me complete this book.

I THE ELEMENTS

*When I was a child, like you, I thought like a child,
and asked how all things began*

Sung from the generation of AIR

or vacancy, what memory can sing

before there is memory

a breath sent into being before

a being

draws in and out

its breath, in darkness

when being,

confettied,

is not yet mote

not beam

not remnant of cloud;

a thin thread of motion

gathering weight

in weightless

space.

There loneliness

leaned into nothing

fell into the world

and was the first

of all things

falling

toward falling.

How the stillness turned

and whistled

and the whistle

was in the wind—

and a pod,

released and rattled,

flew spilled,

then filled with air

a part of air

        in urgency,

     a boundary made by bursting,

  what we call

       the winding of the wind.

The ear is a drum and cavern

          that will not close against the world,

and so we build our houses

         where the wind cannot enter at will

blow the house down

        stall the ship

the wind,

   our enemy,

    runs toward us in the night

      or withholds

at daybreak

    for days

       on end.

I woke to wonder

what if the wind were evil,

the force of an incessant pain

Unbind, unwind the four winds

without them, no direction.

———

Yet air is the element most bearable   most bearable to every mortal thing.

———

the flight

snatched away, the paper lands flat at first,

clings to the cement; the smooth side friction-

-locked to the pitted surface for a second,

then lifted by a corner,

then swirling, then dipping,

flush against the steel of a car door,

then flying off toward a branch,
                              snagged,
unsnagged, sailing

On one side the answers were traced so carefully,

capitals and small letters, peaks and valleys,

a black pen tacking between the blue lines.

Forget the answers, and then the test, and then the paper,

and then the sidewalk, and then the tree, and then the sky—

this is the order of forgetting, the one you already know by heart;

it is neither evil nor good, as things are neither here nor there when they fly

whisper

A whisper within an ordinary parting,
a sigh nesting in a word, it comes
inside another breeze, warmer, softly,
to touch your cheek or shoulder, lighting down
as down does and doesn't and does again.
What was it?
You will ask yourself and you will ask
again until asking itself is like
a caress, nothing then something
and nothing again there in the clear as day,
but something, something meant—
what was it?

the memory of happiness in a time of misery

Like starlings in winter the wind beating against their beating wings
    the air numb and mutely blank a whiteness
      tumbling the dead leaves they too
        whirled like dead leaves torqued
          one way then another for the sake
            of each other even in death joined
              by their scattered dovelike gliding
                two heads bowed above a page
                  the lamp sputtered flickered sparked
                  in the deafening silence
                    the ear is a drum a cavern
                      that will not close against
                        the voice of the beloved and
                        the eye has a door
                          that can bar a whirlwind
                            a sanctuary shut to its harm
                            Scirocco hot dust breaking in the mouth
                          dumb the tongue mute to reason cause
                      an eye held open to see not seeing
                    furled the thought dried to powdery sense
              one way then another for the sake
            of each other even in death joined
          by mistaken heaven's playthings
          gods needless mindless of consequence
        three heads bowed above a page
      an olive stripped bare of its silver
     and a hill stripped bare of its tree
    barren random an iron lung
   bellowing a dark cup thrown
  into the flames
 draw a clearing around the heart
so it might breathe freely again

the survival of Icarus

My father saw the feathers on the waves and grieved
and hadn't heard the voice within the wind
that blew the wax back into form the way
the cold dawn shapes a candle's foam.
I had heard that voice before
in some far time beyond this place
and I think of it now as a living net,
though I do not know how it spans our world
or if it sings from its strings or its spaces.

listen

in a golden field alone

        lone

the quick dust whirling

        hirling

eyes burning

        urning

burning tears. Where

        ere

was the other? Gone

        one

and unknowing, no one

        ne

could answer, crying

        rying

there in desolation

        solation

forgotten

        gotten

forsaken

        saken

for pity

        pity

forbear

        be air

Drawn from the generation of FIRE

Smoke funneling black and back on the wind, a plumed

    negation of the clouds. I was looking for life

        and it welled up, out of the center of the earth,

            deep where flames are freed in flame, shining

                in paradise, burning in hell—where the quick

            and quickest change flies, blazing,

    fast to forever, circled

by the light of living fire.

Smoke funneling black and back on the wind, a plumed
    wand trailing to lace to invisible where the sweeps
        dove down
            brush first
        brittle in the darkness of their limbs.

unloved the poor sent into tunnels, brush-burnt
    flesh torn,
        unloved
                the poor brought down
                the ladders, bruises
                grown black on their lungs

    retrospection, the endrhyme
    of neglect

a red line throbbing on the far horizon—

negation of the clouds. I was looking for life
    all was burning, rising
    hoof-first where the barn door
    imploded, a wild eye
    spinning, a harness clattering.
    You can see and cannot look,
    a wall of flame, stall-pounding,
    smell of hide
    and feathers singed,
    the squealing above,
        the whinnying over lowing

           in March a little redbreast came back
           and a brown chick with a red mark on her tail

and it welled up, out of the center of the earth, on an ordinary day when the ships are at sea and whitecaps speck the bay. The baker inspects his loaves, a dog fetches his ball, the courtesans lean back where the walls are cool and morning lingers in corners cast by shadows. The stars withdrawing now behind the clouds; the sleepers sleeping at the threshold to the forge and the charred bits drifting, sifting on their faces.

It had all happened before, but reasons outrun repetition; disaster in the distance, then fetching fury, coming down from the terraced hills. The plowman, running, reached the city limits. Aflame, he fell into the river's flames.

the blackbirds
     cawing
          weaving
in and out of the ash-dense sky

sleepers at the threshold of the forge still dreaming
sleepers drifting deep below the silt of time

deep where flames are freed in flame, shining
the dead are lit by candlelight
around a gleaming table,
their books lie open,
the pages chosen,
soft lead softly drawn
along the margins like
a whisper

Read to me tonight, tell me what they want to say.
How the yellow glows
in the silver teaspoons, mirroring
their lips and ears and
eyes in longing there,
convex then concave,
their faces shimmering.
I am listening
I am waiting
for your voice
to be carried, electric
on the surface of that light

in paradise, burning in hell—where the quick
are split from the damned, a chaplet of light around their hair or acrid
smart thickening the tongue forever
where the quick fear quickens:

the eye cannot enter the hand cannot touch
element least borne by beings made of water
you must not go alone into that place

and quickest change flies, blazing,

the fennel stalk stolen, a wisp of straw

twig   vine   chips

quick-caught

clever little crimes and then the steady blaze
a meteor *
*

*chinoiserie

**

*chrysanthemums

* showering

**
*

*streams of stars *
*

*

color without quantity, light without measure
the edge never edged until the wick is put out

fast to forever, circled

then you will know the one desire
that pulses through the currents of the heart
drawing desiccating unnerving
heat at the brow and arms and sex
yearning and yearning
through vacant night
the film in the grate
curls twisting to itself
then floats hovers
dips before it shatters

by the light of living fire

all things pulsing are drawn toward the sun

and bound to be unbound from igneous earth

the salamander stirs, the phoenix wings away

and ash sustains the frailest root

Build fires to worship the wood, burn wood to worship the fire

Read to me tonight by the fire,
                         a book is burning in my hands

II SHADOW GEORGICS

I had a little dove
made of paper and string.
I pulled him along behind me—
he could not sing.

He was a made thing.
I made him by heart.
He did not sing at all
and that was all of his art.

Apple

If I could come back from the dead, I would come back
for an apple, and just for the first bite, the first
break, and the cold sweet grain
against the roof of the mouth, as plain
and clear as water.

Some apple names are almost forgotten
and the apples themselves are gone. The smokehouse,
winesap and York imperial, the striped
summer rambo and the winter banana, the little
Rome with its squat rotunda and the pound apple

that pulled the boughs to the ground.
The sheep's nose with its three-pointed snout,
the blue Pearmain, speckled and sugared.
Grime's golden, cortland, and Stayman.
If an apple's called "delicious," it's not.

Water has no substance
and soil has no shell,
sun is all process
and rain cannot rise.
The apple's core carries

a birth and a poison.
Stem and skin, and flesh,
and seed, the apple's name,
no matter, is work
and the work of death.

If you wait for the apple, you wait
for one ripe moment. And should
you sleep, or should you dream, or
should you stare too hard in the daylight
or come into the dark to see

what can't be seen, you will drop
from the edge, going over into
coarse, or rot, or damping off.
You will wake to yourself, regretful,
in a grove of papery leaves.

You need a hillside, a small and steady wind,
a killing frost, and, later, honeybees.
You need a shovel, and shears, and a ladder

and the balance to come back down again.
You will have fears of codling moths
and railroad worms, and aphids.

Scale and maggots and beetles
will come to do their undoing.
Forests will trap the air

and valleys will bend to gales—
cedars will bring on rust, so keep them
far in the distance. Paradise,

of course, was easy, but you and I live
in this world, and "the fruit of the tree
in the midst of the garden"

says nothing specific about apples;
the "apples of gold" in Proverbs
are probably oranges instead.

And so are the fruits
Milanion threw down:
an apple does not glitter.

If you're interested in immortality
it's best to plant a tree, and even
then you can't be sure that form

will last under weather.
The tree can break apart in a storm
or be torqued into pieces over many

years from the weight of its ruddy labor.
The state won't let you burn the wood
in the open air; the smoke is too dense

for breathing. But apple-wood
makes a lovely fire, with excellent
heat and aroma.

Fire will take in whatever it can
and heat will draw back
into earth. "Here is the fruit,
your reward and penalty
at once," said the god

to the waiting figures.
Unbearable, the world
that broke into time.
Unbearable, the just-born
certainty of distance.

You can roast late apples
in the ashes. You can run
them in slices on a stick.
You can turn the stem to
find the letter of your love

or chase them down with
your chin in a tub.
If you count the seeds to tell
the future, your heart will
sense more than your

tongue can say. A body
has a season, though
it may not know it,
and damage will bloom
in beauty's seed.

If I could come back from the dead, I would—
I'd come back for an apple,
and just for one bite, one break,
and the cold sweet grain on the tongue.
There is so little difference between

an apple and a kiss, between desire
and the taste of desire.
Anyone who tells you other-
wise is a liar, as bad
as a snake in the quiet grass.

You can watch out for the snake and the lie.
But the grass, the green green wave
of it, there below the shadows of the black
and twisted boughs, will not be
what you thought it would be.

Bees

That the bees were born in the corpse of the injured animal.
That the bees came forth out of the corrupted flesh.

That a small room was chosen, made narrow just for this,
and the animal was led beneath the low roof and cramped walls

and that the four winds came through the four windows
and that the morning fell upon the small

and heavy head, its horns curving out
from the whorled medallion of the forehead.

That the hot nostrils and the breathing mouth were stopped
and the flesh was beaten, pounded to a pulp,
beneath the unbroken hide.

      He lies on his side on the broken apple-boughs. He lies on a bed
    of fragrant thyme and the cassia is laid in sprays about him
and the sweetness of the fields surrounds him.

Do this when the west winds blow. Do this when the meadows
are alive with poppies. Do this when the swallow hangs her pendulous

nest and the dew is warm and the days grow long.
And all the living fluids will swirl within the hide, and the bones

will dissolve like bread in water.
And a being will be born, and another, and then a thousand

and a thousand thousand swarming without limbs or form.
And that the wings will grow from atoms. And that the stirring wings

will find their way into the air. And that a thousand stirring wings
will come forth into the day like a storm of arrows made of wind

and light. And the flesh will fall back into the earth, and the horror
into sweetness and the dark into the sun and the bees
thus born.

—VIRGIL, *Georgics,* Book IV.281–314

Braid

Shoulders knobbed against
a slat-backed chair,
the temples tugged, a pull

at the nape, you felt the up-
sweep as she smoothed the fine
wisps back and tucked

yank into yank
and a third into that
until the consecutive

dodges of thumbs and first
fingers gathered,
fraying and filing

to their end—ended
in an ornament that, suspended,
looked ridiculous, even

on a child who mostly
set forth with
what was called

a "finished" look, some
loose ends in order
where others were not

and a slight weight below
the nape's pull. The view
others had of it

was invisible to you.
It made something there
where there would have been

a blank—now instead
a kind of face
sent from woman to

woman like a duty,
an obstinate
duty to pattern.

It's too simple to see
one thing rather
than another, a wish

protruding once it's been
suppressed, a vise that holds
a thought in its proper

place until it bobs
to the surface
of a generally balmy

sea. Women and
woman only a letter
away—a strand gets

mixed, then mixed
right out of the heaven
of perfect fit;

one kind of accident
turns into another.
The whole head throbs for days.

Black and white are woven
into gray the way
hyperbole has no chance

once it's juxtaposed
to reason—negation
just a thread among

the available options
and hope itself apparent
there in the very

notion a made thing can last.
Tougher, coarser, split
weave in the years. Shorter,

longer, shorter, the brain
bound to its anchor.
The brushed-out waves

with their rick-rack
shadows, a thread
inside the case,

the case inside
the locket, the locket
beneath the yoke.

All the effort
to save in itself
a form of loss.

You can tell a story
many ways. You can leave
something out or put

something in; you can fool
yourself and hide.
You can shake out

the form or try
to manage every wisp,
but the latter will

only bring you pain.
You went under
the hand and eye of another

and the tether cannot
be undone.

Cross/X

"Don't look cross-eyed at me like that."
I buried the doll with a nail in her waistband
and marked the spot with a stone.

"Don't look cross-eyed at me like that."
I buried the doll with a nail in her waistband
and marked the spot with a stone.

(not foreseeing that stones could move, could be kicked aside by a hoof or a
wheel or worn away by storms, that a censor could come from the world and
not only from the need to forget . . . .

    Often, when you want to know what childhood was like, I think of that
doll with her broken eye and its vexing mechanical twinkle, of the cavernous
seams of her plastic body, the correct numbers of her fingers and toes, her three
separate outfits for three occasions.

    Something awful in the idea of occasion, something dressed out even in
her nakedness.

    Everyone knows that dolls are uncanny; the smallest child can tell
they're worse than ghosts. You spend your love on them day after day and they
teach you the meaning of *unrequited.* On a whim, they fall apart or outlive you,
and all the while you'll think the whim's your own.

    I had wrapped her in a hurry in her party dress and apron. The nail was
a sixpenny flat head, so new it shone in the sunlight. Did I think she could use
it in an afterlife? Was it a totem or rebus, meant to *nail* her identity, to fix for
once and all just who or what she was?

A stone, a nail, a cross-eyed look: X marks the spot, then weather mars the X. I knew about *pirates* and *resurrections*. I must have been hopping mad.

You could try to find her; she's somewhere on the latitude of the fence and the silo, the longitude of the barn and the shed. But if you do, you'll only have the real thing she's become—no longer a lie, but the truth of a lie, a plastic fact below the hard-packed dirt. Just another place where something happened, something no one else remembers, and that, in remembering, I am burying once again, marking with these marks that will not stay. In the end, there were three occasions: mica, feldspar, and clay.)

Dark the star

Dark the star
deep in the well,
bright in the still
and moving water,
still as the night
circling above
the circle of stones
the darkness surrounds.
Dark the wish
made on the star,
a true wish made
on the water's image.

There's no technique in the grass.
There's no technique in the rose.

Ellipse

Night after night the astronomer
     imagined the stars in their orbits,
          building his orrery of glass and string;

       he was making a kind of singing
     that came from far beyond
himself, beyond the sounds
     that human mouths will bring
          into a form of being.

       And then, one night,
     it came to him
that the circles and spheres
     had no meaning—that,
          spinning, the globe's center

       might not return, ever,
     to its point of beginning.
Instead a new circle
     was entwined there and
          another, and another—

until each was traversed
and described in its path.
It seemed to be the way the thread
a silkworm drops is thrown
around itself,

building a kind of house from
the weaving of so many
small orbits, drawn out
from the center on one side
and drawn in from the other,

producing an uneven motion,
alternately fast and lingering.
It was late, and reading
about the astronomer,
you thought grief could take

a shape like this. You thought
a loop, placed, then displacing,
could wind around and around
as each turn verged farther
from its start, plying its motion

without a given rhythm—all
things following from diminishment,
all things following a weighted
spin until you could not
bear to return to where

the loss, your loss, had been.
While you sat reading, late
into the night, someone was
setting a table, someone was
packing with slow precision.

The quiet metals—a fork, a spoon—
lay on the snowy cloth.
Someone turned down the sound
and it backed once more into silence.
Leaving your book, you came

into the room just as a door
in the distance was closing;
the surface of the table,
you realized, was still warm
from where a hand had been

resting. And you saw
how the room was like a clearing
in a forest; the brambles fell away
and the vault of sky appeared—the kind
of story you were told again

and again in the years before
you could read. You had half-
heard those words, like the thoughts
of someone sewing, or someone
compelled by bright flowers to

wander deeper
and deeper from
the road toward home.
You could not be more alone
in that place

that was the source
of all your forgetting.
And then you recalled how
the saint had said that
a body tends to follow

its own weight, its own weight
to its own place, not always
downward, not always toward
the earth, but to its own place
like fire rising upward.

If the lights of the heavens
were to cease, he said,
if the potter's wheel continued
to be turning, all things would go
to their own place and the sun

and the moon and the stars,
as well, would follow the time
of returning to their places,
the time that no one yet knows.
You came into a room that turned into

             a clearing and the clearing bore
        outward like an eye. Oil beneath
water rises over water; fire on
        the water is carried upward.
                  Things in their order seem to be

                  at rest, but are moving toward
        their places with an inner fire
and weight. You thought you
        were singing the song of the orrery,
                  where all things follow the motion

                  of light. But the stars are perfect;
        we do not live among them.
We do not know them and
        cannot know them; their music
                  steals the senses

                  and slows us into sleep.
        You were moving with a purpose,
though you did not know it yet.
        You were moving like a sleeper
                  through the shoals

                  of night. And that is how you
        found this place; you cradled
one ear against the sky and put the other
        against the ground. You chose your form
                  of leaning: you chose to stop and fall.

Forms of Forts

Hay Fort

A labyrinth. A pencil shaft of light
wherever four bales couldn't squarely meet.
The twine tight, lifting as abrading.

A twinge, the prickly collar rubbing
a scratching rash along the forearm.
The heaviness of the hay in the hot dark.

So earnestly, we set
to building for ourselves.
That there should be something
where before there was nothing.

Then the fervent hours
of catching and pretending,
the dreaming hours of strings
and lucky stones.

If you touch one of your hands
with another, the one that touches
will seem alive, the other like
an object to be awakened.

When winter ended,
the doors were rolled back and the broad day
flooded the loft.
And then we could see, in the swath

of sunlight, the stray clover bud,
or jewelweed, or fireweed
or evening primrose,
or robin's plantain,

Thistle, or chicory,
even once great mullein—
the leaf that's called
velvet dock.

Whatever had been in the mower's path
was bound and pressed into the hay.

You cannot know both hands at once;
you must choose between the living and the dead.

A labyrinth broken open from above
or worn away at its foundations.

That there might be something when there is nothing
and the source of light confused with holiness.

Snow Fort

Come in, come here, come into
this place that's been made for us,
that was packed and braced for us
against the collapsing rain.
Come in, it's a cavern in the white
heart of the sea. Come in
where the silence is like breathing
moonlight, where a faint taste
of iodine will lie on your lips
and you'll never be cold again.
In every part of space, there is another part of space.
When this is gone, it will not disappear.

Let me tell you about my marvelous god

Let me tell you about my marvelous god, how he hides in the hexagons
of the bees, how the drought that wrings its leather hands
above the world is of his making, as well as the rain in the quiet minutes
that leave only thoughts of rain.
An atom is working and working, an atom is working in deepest
night, then bursting like the farthest star; it is far
smaller than a pinprick, far smaller than a zero and it has no
will, no will toward us.
This is why the heart has paced and paced,
will pace and pace across the field where yarrow
was and now is dust. A leaf catches
in a bone. The burrow's shut by a tumbled clod
and the roots, upturned, are hot to the touch.
How my god is a feathered and whirling thing; you will singe your arm
when you pluck him from the air,
when you pluck him from that sky
where grieving swirls, and you will burn again
throwing him back.

Two Brief Views of Hell

Leaving the fringe of light at the edge of the leaves, deep then deeper,
the rocking back and forth movement forward through the ever-narrowing circle
that never, in truth, narrowed beyond the bending going in,
not knowing whether a turn or an impasse would lie at the place
where the darkness turned into impenetrability, deep where
no longer could down or up or side to side be known, just the effort
to stay above the water, to keep one spread palm bearing
against the weight and then the other, deeper and deeper.
The way in was easy once it began. The way in was all necessity.
Behind the darkness, more darkness; beneath the water only water.

A great black frayed trash bag lifted by the wind high above the sidewalk,
then just above the roofs, a black shining sail tattered, too big to be flying
and yet, each time it began its descent, lifted, propped up
and stiffened again in a sequence of small swirling movements.
The most oppressive thing,
the most tormenting, a black sun deflated, teasing,
touching the cornices and windows, block after block,
a hovering force, a curse, a smear.
The farther it rose in the distance, the larger it seemed to loom.
The mind wants an object and then recoils at what it has done.

The mind wants an object and then recoils at what it has done.
The farther it rose in the distance, the larger it seemed to loom.
A hovering force, a curse, a smear
touching the cornices and windows, block after block,
the most tormenting, a black sun deflated, teasing,
the most oppressive thing
and stiffened again in a sequence of small swirling movements
and yet, each time it began its descent, lifted, propped up
then just above the roofs, a black shining sail tattered, too big to be flying
A great black frayed trash bag lifted by the wind high above the sidewalk.

Behind the darkness, more darkness; beneath the water only water.
The way in was easy once it began. The way in was all necessity
against the weight and then the other, deeper and deeper
to stay above the water, to keep one spread palm bearing
no longer could up or down or side to side be known, just the effort
where the darkness turned into impenetrability, deep where
not knowing whether a turn or an impasse would lie at the place
that never, in truth, narrowed beyond the bending going in,
the rocking back and forth movement forward through the ever-narrowing circle.
Leaving the fringe of light at the edge of the leaves, deep then deeper.

shadow / Isaiah

I will bring again the shadow of the degrees, which is gone down in the sun-dial
of Ahaz. . . . So the sun returned ten degrees, by which degree it was gone down.
                                                                    —*Isaiah 38:8*

In the book of Isaiah,
God saves a man's life
by pushing back a sun-dial's
shadow exactly
ten degrees.
That night when you were inconsolable,
damp with fever and pain
and cried until
your cry was gone,
you, too, needed ten degrees
for the white blood cells to stop
their milling frenzy,
for the infant ticking of your brain
to go on.
And just as at noontime on a beach
in summer a shadow will fall
all at once on the sand
from a slip of cirrus that arrives
out of nowhere, then goes back,

a stray wisp, into the blue,
they were granted.
For everything has its countering
shadow, everything
under the sun. The aspens
shaking down
the light and the gorges
cut, swirling,
by freezing, then
thawing, all shiver
with the same
fevered motion that quaked
through your own small
shoulders and teeth—
it's just a matter of scale,
or at least that's what
I used to think
until I had a glimpse of
the other side of mercy,
which is mercy withheld
like the rain—
when the green coursing
below the bark can't reach
the shrunken buds, and the brackish
water blows away,
and the corn browns,
stunted, in the fields.
Then the dying can yearn
for death, though death
isn't ready
to collect its due:
that's when I saw

that the sphere of luck
is smaller than the sphere of mirrors
and the sphere of mirrors smaller,
much smaller,
than the steel face of the sea.

Jump

A moth
lives inside
the seed—viz.,
it's true, you can love
the invisible the livelong
day and night after night sealed
up in it, too, dazzled by
the never, by what
will never be
seen,

or you can go the other way,

with your beak under your wing,
that keeps you from the air,
your first breath, starting to peep,
the inside out,
You'll tap and tap the star pip
the egg-tooth
its meaning entirely
you'll make a hole
the light, even though
what light might be.
like a troubled
for hours around
until the whole
breaks open and falls
that's when seeing
every star a planet, every

and press against the membrane
until it breaks and you can take
sounding deep within
a mistake switching into a purpose.
with the small point on your bill,
made just for this,
its use. And gradually
that grows to let in
you won't yet know, can't know,
Then you'll twist and turn
dreamer, orbiting
the circuit of your wall
large end of the shell
into pieces all about you—
will be believing:
planet realigned.

Kingfisher Carol

*halcyon—a period of calm weather which exists during the seven days
preceding and the seven days following the shortest day of the year; so
called from a nautical tradition that the halcyon, or kingfisher, builds her
nest on the water and that in spite of the violent weather prevalent at this
time, the gods grant a respite from all storms while she hatches and rears
her young.*

Star for the shepherds,
star for the kings
and the kingfishers
perched on the waves.
On the halcyon sea,
they nest their nests
from twigs
and briars and hay.

Jars of myrrh
and silver caskets
locked with
golden keys,
eastern starlight
trailing eastward,
the manger
piled with sheaves.

Pelt and steam
in a timbered stable,
the kings fall on
their knees;
shepherds lean
on their staves to doze
and dream
of meadows and leas.

The light shines
there in the desert dark
and the darkness
knows it not,
shines on the flocks
and the towered walls,
on the throne
and the narrow cot.

Star for the kings,
star for the shepherds,
the kingfishers sing
from the waves.
On the halcyon sea,
they nest their nests
from twigs and briars
and hay.

Lightning

Was it the god of mercy or the god of light
    who calmed the water—glasswater,
        as far as the eye could see,
          and held the wind
          within its pen,
  and hid the first sounds of thunder
        behind the rumbling trucks on the bridge?

And was it the god of mercy or the god
of light who showered down
    the ions that
        stilled
        and sparked
           the air, expanding, flashing in the far
              horizon like flecks
          of silver—a thousand,
          then thousands—
  until the very distance vanished
        into gleam and floating weeds?

And which god was it, mercy or light,
    who blacked out all the blue,
        who sent the rain hammering
          in waves across the waves,

close and closer, just in reach,
            then directly overhead,
                        stinging
to ricochet, sharp
            at every angle,
                        while the water crept into the bow?

Then which god steadied the oars in their rhythm
            and which one crabbed and plucked them?

And which one held out the bridge as a refuge,
            while the other shoved the shell
                        into the roiling current?

            (a carp was leaping by the island;
                        the cormorant rested on a sagging rope, one wing pulled
                                    up and over like a blanket)

Because now what I really need to know
            is the name of the god who rent that darkness,

                        who came running with his knife
                                    and tore the jagged line,

            then held up the tear
                        a bristling instant,

            (suspended in the static,
a racing frantic clicking)

                        and exposed the quick white
radiance inside.

Who was that god who ripped into the world
then came no closer, closing his ambition—
        combing it, smoothing it
back, diminished,
        sending soon
                a quiet rain?

Was it the one who bears down in fury
        and demands to be paid in kind

or the one who buoys and swells
        from below as he lifts the boat backward to the dock—

the god of mercy, moored to the earth,
or the god of light, married to pain?

This is what I need to know
and it won't be a god who will tell me

shadow/ Lintel

I stood before the lintel;
       the door swung open then.
Your name was there, and mine,
       and the date of every birth—

All was clear as day,
       but they could not bring me in.

Beyond another door
       and then another, endless more
though the distance had
been measured in the dust—
       one print stepping
       after another
       and none of them
       turning back
       to us.

What You Said about the Moon

All the little lies follow the big lie
while the big lie is pared away.

Fading face, old friend
of my left hand waning,
of my right hand waxing:
gibbous mirror womb for womb.

Throbbing pulse and dangling watch,
globing, shrinking, hinged
where night
unhinges night.

Cause of eloquence
ending in derangement.

There could be such a thing as too much feeling.

I had meant to harvest, not to hunt.

Turn your money over,
blow ashes,
whisper "I saw you before you saw me."

Night Songs

*

Oleander, pennywort
a fillip in the wind
breath blows ash across the sill
comes from the tarnished cup.

*

Hobo trills his acid flute
opossum snouts the leaves
oak-dry, gold-lit motes fly up
and up, now spark, now out.

*

Shrew-run, shrew-struck
owl and gem-eyed beetle
glitter curls between the teeth
nails scrape furrowed bark.

*

Where the wind lays down her head
sirens swell the sound
the redwood's wands are woven up
and back through liquid limbs.

*

Gate locked, turnstile stopped
shuttered, curtained, blind
the cutworm, slug, and aphid
soon shred the petalled stem.

*

Bonfire or barnfire
accident or not
pain's a form of telescope
for watchers on the hill.

*

Instruments of interval
calibrated space
physician's glove inside the chest
a cave of mineral cold.

*

Pacing waiter, pacing, waits
Patrons loiter, linger
fingering the button bank
where star-lit codes will flicker.

*

Love's not love in video
charmed beasts go extinct
song's not song unless it's stung
with static, scat, and ink.

＊

Night sweats, nicotine and sweet
syringe, rehearsal, fear
cheap life, cheaper now than ever
leaping on a dare.

＊

Nicotiana, honey-bloomer,
trumpeting awaft
satin-edged and rustling
in fluorescent milky light.

＊

Gunman scratches itching palm
drinker staggers glass
brown bag sheaths the sorry lip
headlights pass and pass.

＊

Raisins, almonds, little lambs,
fox has gone ahunting
butterflies pecking eyes—
sleep before the haunting.

＊

Carousels of janitors
—door revolving still—
grab the ring when you come round
take the cord and pull.

*

Melancholy Saturn, sad-
sack St. Jerome
skulls that pull all-nighters
redcaps trudging home.

*

Neon clouds fill shopping malls
ashen crowds assemble,
angels under wheels of fire
where dream and dread are moved.

*

Mauve and black and monochrome
taste and hear and touch
(vision stays empirical)
harm's way stands unknowing.

*

St. George took his shuteye
that bound up every wound,
brittle brakes and membrane webs
around his sickness wound.

*

Moon swings low above the sink
Dog Star gone forgetting
frost has barbed the hawthorn's
thorn again and tinged the grass.

*

Resolution wanders
rage slips from its edge
foxglove checks the ferns with red
where woodbine binds the bank.

*

Cloud and moon and cloud
again; old moon in her arms
wing has gone to forage
where sedges spring abreast.

*

Cereus and spiderwort
alight the blearest wind
that ever blew across the sill
come drink now, drink it in.

Now in the minute

Now in the minute, in the half-life when the rose

    light lights the high leaves, rises,

and then the sun itself appears, when

    the shadow at the back of something like

a thought, implacable, still clouds,

    what, what is it? The vaguely milky half-light,

a tick or jolt—*what was it?*

    Now goes sun over wood, over antennae—

belt on the shoe, dust on the glass: a mote

    (motet, motel?)

        fades, as the lens pulls back

and the mind's screen blurs: news that isn't

    exactly news.

        You tell me your

dream and I'll tell you mine.

The wire-

wheeled crib in the attic, the acorns clustered

in the rusted tin: "We had another child

and forgot all about it—we'd forgotten

it, left it, in the crib in the attic,

for months or days."

Ridiculous—how could

you forget? How could anyone forget?

The swaddling unwrapped,

unwrapped, unravelled; the wife of Lot came back,

—no *Lazarus* came back. The prodigal

son came back, the quarreling squirrels

are what you heard. It wasn't the teeth

falling out, all the classical worries—

musty, dumped, ineffable. Laughable.

And yet the moral horror might drag

on and on as it does in the dream of the drifting

boat, the idyll of the two on the slate-dark

water; something snags as the sleepers

fall deeper into sleep and the dreamer

who watches is helpless to wake them.

Are you half as happy as they are, or half
as happy as even that?

The dove sang who whoo
along the hard path
at twilight each star
alone seemed a sign.
Nothing was joined,
nothing was lost.
Others in line
lifted their hands.
Some seemed to pray
some seemed to dance.
The dove sang who whoo
along the hard path.
I looked for you,
but you were gone.

Now that the world's contracted thus, the cover
thrown off to *where*—where are we now?
Do you call that a nightmare or a wish?
Saying so doesn't make it so.

I saw in the diminishment of every

living thing the radiance of its end.

I heard in the interval, in the intake

of your breath, the cell's pulse, the quick

and mortal pendulum.

You tell me my

dream and I'll tell you yours.

The fleck and the pool, the bright stain,

obdurate,

       left by the too-long

look at the sun—there in your eyes

I saw what lingers.

I awakened to the world as it was given.

O

Toi, toi, toi, said Peleus.
Grieving, Hecuba
barked like a dog.
O said the woman
who spoke only English,
who cast an English
zero out, a wreath
on the battering waves.
O the teeth clenched.
O a fistful of hair.

Pear

Believing each simple thing passes from a perception that is less clear
into one that is, eventually, more clear. Believing each simple thing contains

within it a minimal unity beyond which whatever else can be
exists. That the two seeds, or four seeds, are where the pear will go and where

it began. Black bark, blossoms in the mild rain, smelling like piss
in the spring rain, the chips and twigs raining down beneath our weight

as we broke off bouquets for the teacher. "What is that smell?" she asked.
Stark, white, delicate, attached with green cuffs,

twig to twig, the blooms bursting through the runnels that
held them. Five runnels made in the foil by five fingers.

The given world is infinite and reality is complete.

That's what I had written in the morning on the blackboard.
And then, going home, I was stalled

again on the bridge. I looked up and out and there
I saw the girl flying and falling, flying and falling

in the distance, in the narrow air between two buildings,
her arms outspread, over and over

against the strip of sky and above the gravel, or grass
or ground—the light changed and I couldn't see at all

where or how she had dragged the trampoline
that must have been the yielding source of all her motion.

If you find a sight like this a kind of gift or sign, you've missed the way
the mind seals over, the way the simplest thing pulls on its heavy hood

and turns away slowly from a thought. For later, weeks later,
I was stalled again in mid-bridge and couldn't remember,

yet could vaguely remember, the sense that something
was about to happen, that the light

would change like a bell or alarm
and that in turn would mean the time had come

when everyone must leave the school—
with every sweater and pencil left in place

—to burn, and burn
and burn back to the ground.

The History of Quiver

His arrowes he wore in a Woolues skinne
all at his back for his Quiver.

Fair Virgin Huntress, for the Chace array'd
with painted Quiver and unerring Bow

His quaver he Hung in one silver lace.

The taper'd Dart, design'd to make
his Quiver in my heart.

Bow of my life, then yet thou art full
of Spring and my quiver
hath many purposes.

Nay, if Cupid have not spent
all his Quiver in Venice,
thou wilt quake for this shortly,

quiver in Venice.

Your bright eyes carry a quiver of darts
within them,
sharper than sunbeams.

Thrasymachus, I said, with a quiver,
have mercy on us,
quote mercy.

Heaven was grand with the quiver—
the quiver of its many living fires.

Of body feeble and impotent, but of soule
quick and lustie, a-quiver.

Thy quick and quiver wings.

A little quiver fellow.

Thy galling shafts lye quivered in my bones

as Dido quyvered and shoke of grete rage.

O'er the dying lamp th'unsteady flame Hangs quivering

and the gales then quivered among the branches.

The quiver of its many living fires.

Upon the stream the moonbeams quiver;
the quivering moonbridge on the quick black stream

Cast not a sheep's eye Upon the quivering of my calf.

A soft paued lodging for quivering Goates.

His tapered dart, the Bow of my Life.
Unerring life on a silver lace.

The silver quivering of the element.

Electricity: A wide brush of pale ramifications,
having a quivering motion.

Rewind

Strange how he had written, when he was thinking about music,
        that it is not motion, but a miracle, if a thing changes

place without crossing the interval
        between its former and latter place.

Like a sequence of sounds, the path a thing follows
        traces an unbroken line and then the line

becomes the mark of a motion. And he realized
        that no one goes from one place to another

without traversing all the intervening
        places. Motion closes the space

between places without
        interruption or hesitation.

That was something he knew to be certain.
        For motion, a thing changing

place is continuous—continuous in time.
        And all things refer to the motion of bodies.

All things join the ceaseless music of sequence.
        Nature, he thought, makes no jumps.

But he was a writer who was given to forgetting, and as
        he opened the seducer's diary, he read how a girl

will take a running start, how "her leap
        is a floating. Young, newborn, like a flower

shooting up from the root of a mountain."
        The girl was swaying, so reckless,

at the summit, and everything turned
        black before his eyes.

He could imagine her running as a kind of game,
        but the diary said, "an unfolding

of grace." A running start,
        it said, separates a girl and a man:

"For a young girl a leap is just
        a leap, while a man's leap becomes

something ridiculous. No matter how widely
        he reaches and strives, his exertion turns out

to be nothing compared to the distance
        between the crags. He's little more

than a yardstick—that's why we call this place
        'The Maiden's Leap.'"

Inert as the page on which it was written, the thought
        of the seducer was tangled, caught

around the girl's leaping image.
        He said she jumps

in a different way. He said, wherever she
        turns, the infinite surrounds her,

yet the "infinite comes as easily
        to a girl as the conception that all

love must be happy."
        And for a while the writer was taken in

by the craggy picture and yawning abyss,
        by the terror of those spaces where a girl

"cannot follow the hard,
        the difficult, way of thought."

        Then, coming to his senses, he remembered
once more the certainty—the closing

        of the interval; he saw at last
how the aspect of ecstasy could lie

        in the chance of leaving the line.
And that is the moment where I have left him,

        the moment I am running toward.
After all, it is dark—

dark in that place and dark in this one
—and the darkness continues into darkness

like the ceaseless sequence of music.
The aspect of ecstasy lies in leaving the line.

It's dark,
so for God's sake don't jump.

The Rose

Not so long ago, or was it?—the bud was tightly wound and the edge
as hard to start as a roll of cellophane tape
      (though it wasn't up to you or me to start it)

Remember how the "dew and velvet" first caught our eye?
      how the butter-yellow striations went
            into pink, or withdrew from pink?

(though it wasn't up to you or me to say which way it was going)

The corolla did unfurl. The anther cracked and flew.
      Each part in fact played its part, and when we turned away,
          it didn't die—of course, or not
             because of that.

Eventually, it shattered
     like any rose, just as roses do:
        first the outer
           petals, then the inner ones that cling
             a little longer
               to the pistil,

though even that wasn't the end, for the hip
had hardly begun—its apple-green knob
would still take months
to ripen and wither

—the very months that send
        their filaments toward the sun:
                the *long ago,* the *start,*
                        the *little longer, eventually,*
                                the *end* like clockwork—notions
        drawn from simple math, like *clockwork.*

When you and I are gone, it's true
that time will die in time.
It won't be up to the rose
to say which way
the wind has blown.

        I was wandering alone in u ruin
        as vast . . . as vast as the moon . . .
        and thought that time
        had a form of its own,
        but then the rose came to save me.

Scarecrow

Now, when I picture him, I realize his secret
    was that he had no secret.

    The whole summer long he lived
        less than a life
            and more than the existence
                that is granted to objects.

    He resembled a place and a person at once,
        his getup first fit for a hoedown,

        then bleached by weeks of sun and rain
            until denim was done in, tattersall
                fell into checkered tatters.

Under the straw hat, instead of a face,
    there was only the notion of a look,

    something steady, still,
        when all the living world

        knew fear as
            an atmosphere of presence.

The sun at noon and the moon effaced by clouds, the wind
in the shocks and the light

on the leaves, a mouse
nosing a chipped cob,
        a beetle climbing around a thorn—

these moved as if they were meant to move

        while the crows,
                toward whom his being was bent, read

his immobility
        as a form of intention.

Hair-trigger,
        lime-twig, rusted
saw-tooth on a spring:

a crow's mind can never reach
        the point of not
                really minding.

He was a figure on a stick and the stick stuck
        in the ground; no one

                would have named him or offered
                any thanks—

                anthropomorphizing is what crows do.

The gods do not have bodies and souls;
      they have only their radiant bodies.

         They are perfect and have no sense
           of their perfection.

He couldn't slow or die, would not
      return to earth. Seedy, seeded,
         he was scattered by the wind, scattered

helter-skelter
       by the raking wind.

We built his heir
         from the rag-pile and the straw
           that fell from the loosened sheaves.

You don't have to believe to know
      how such a scene can happen:

     how nature depends
        upon its image of our errors

       and how we, in making what takes place
         in our absence, find some part of ourselves
        that does not grow.

The Seasons

Ice-jammed hard-clasped branches in the blocks a whole river of them
       yet at the same time, the time sensed
beneath the time walked, the time breathing in and out, the water almost
       eddying, still pushing there beneath
the milk-white surface, deep down and over the bed of rocks; you could call
       them frozen, though they never live
another state than less and less until they're gone, the water going on and on
       until it all accrues again. The seasons
always seemed to be a form of freedom, something good for making meaning,
       the kind of notion a founding father could
pull out now and then whenever
       the now and then would flag. Time
healing time, you know the saw.
       Lightning strikes and struck.
The shepherd fell down dead.
And then it all wound up again: a redbreast made a ruckus, the quick eternal sprung.

You wanted summer or you wanted death.
So death came again, and that was autumn.

shadow/ Shadow

You came upon me like a shadow
    and you came into me like a shadow
        and there you dwelled within me
        and I in you;
we were cast on the black water—
    we were cast by the will of the wind
        —then drawn onto the darker
shore where no things grow
    and the dry leaves gather
        and we cannot recognize
        the forms of light.

From "Lessons from Television"

You must laugh at yourself, laugh and laugh.
Music swells the emotions;
music exists to punctuate seeing.
Emotion, therefore, is punctuation.

Formless, freedom resembles abasement.
Abasement is as infinite as desire.
You must laugh at yourself, laugh and laugh.

Those who are not demons are saints.
You are not a demon or a saint.

Women are small and want something,
so laugh at yourself, laugh and laugh.

Beds are sites of abasement.
The news is about the news.

Faces in close-up are always in anguish.
Hair and teeth are clues to class.

Clothes are changing,
changing up or down
And change itself is a laugh.

Cause can't be figured
and consequence is yet to come.

You're either awake or asleep
and that, too, is a clue to class.

Children are never with groups of children
unless they are singing in chorus.

Their mothers cannot do enough,
though there's always room for improvement.

And improvement lies in progress,
though collapsing is good for a laugh.

Saints will turn to the worse.
Demons die if they can be found.

Nature is combat, weather is sublime.
Even weather can make you laugh.

People you don't know are louder than you are,
but what is far away cannot harm you—

Books are objects, families are inspiring.
Animals protect their young;
the young come with the territory.

English is the only language.
Reading is an occasion for interruption,
and interruption is a kind of laugh.

Something is bound to get better.
And there is a pill with your name on it.

When indoors, stick with your own race—
that way you'll feel free to laugh.

Strangers are paying attention to your smell.
A camera will light like a moth on disaster.
Pity will turn to irony.

The street is a dark and frightful place.
Fires are daily.

Your car is your face.

You must laugh at yourself, laugh and laugh.

These Trees in Particular

*I frequently tramped eight or ten miles through the deepest snow to
keep an appointment with a beech-tree, or a yellow birch, or an old
acquaintance among the pines.*

—THOREAU, *Walden,* Winter Visitors

*How the pines shake! Pines are the hardest sort of tree to live when shifted
to any other soil, and here there's none but the crew's cursed clay.*

—MELVILLE, *Moby Dick*

Three pine masts lodged in the clay of the pining sailors.
You can't move the trees and expect them to grow.

Born with the elm, you will die with it.

A beech axle splintered by fury.
Ash for the bat and birch for the arrow.
An olive in the teeth stops the teeth.

Acorns pour down after the drought, up all night from
the rat-a-tat-a-tat. You get a straight story from an oak

and afterwards, disarming silence.
Black yew, black cypress,
widow's weeds will follow.

Poplar and willow, weak by the water.
Swamp maple, weak at heart.

In the shade of the planetree, they'll listen to stones
all day, provided they tell the truth.

If the trees are unfamiliar, you're the stranger.

The chestnut will never come back.

Keep your myrrh in a holly cupboard,
the laurel wreath on a hook by your door,

make the door from the planks
of the broken table, and the table
from the planks of the broken floor.

Dress the fir's amber wound with the tar brush.

Hang suet and seeds for the waxwing.

When you recognize the trees, you must be home.

Unless and Until

Every morning begins like musical chairs
an oldie's spinning,
the MC's cheerful: the backstage
gets crowded with Miracles or
All-Stars, Supremes,
Temptations, or Impressions.
Then by nightfall the seats are gone
and the laughter has a cruel strain
of its own.
You look around and wonder
at the string of progressions,
the trash in the corners that grew into ailanthus,
and all those new trains
rusting fast to their tracks.
There was an errand to be done,
someone needed a present,
ambition had the look
of a shiny bucket;
it was easier to be specific
than to keep in mind the picture
and by then the picture had changed.
And now it's numbing, this sense of the real
that comes weighted down
by the need to have things,
not quite knowing how many

will do, or where to put them,
or how to fix them.
The look of it all becomes so polished
before the replacements arrive,
then something must be done
about the rest who can't, or won't,
surrender their claims to space.
The main goal is to be going faster,
flurrying time into a sort of snowy
pile—what's due is recorded
in the records and only later
can be cashed in for cash.
You can roll up your sleeves
for the cleanup, but others from the start
were cut out for that work.
You'll find yourself left
with your good intentions while
they'll be out of a job.
Catastrophes come in a series,
and over time the series
starts to look like nature;
the worst will be swept
right under the table, and that was the game
they had in mind.
But why try to spare you the ideal when by now
the ideal is who you are?
Rather than chipping at it day after day,
you might as well
go ahead and gather,
letting everything
cling like burrs on a scam—refrains
as persistent as your own
fierce will and in themselves

still next to nothing.
It's your field, your fence;
you've got a grip on all
the systems that underlie the system.
The dreams of reformation
that once pulled us forward have been
set up in the hallways
as sad dioramas.
Even so, I'd like to walk
through that wood again with you
where the sweet underbrush was waiting,
where necessity had a definite form
like the rain, or a roadblock,
or a so-called act of god.
We had forged a path there
for years on end, cutting back
the brambles of *unless*
and *unless,* stripping off
the low thorns of *until* before,
or after—I can't remember now—
something somehow
called us away.

Lost Rules of Usage

period
a tollbooth   a jammed F sharp
footprints leading onto rock

question
a noble brow above the missing lips

comma
red willow leaf
        suspended in the water
an eyelash gone astray on a cheek

colon
adhesive tape mending
        the bridge of your sunglasses

semicolon
a knot and a stain in the plywood
some people can't make up their minds

dash
might as well die trying

exclamation
the slim clown leaping over the ball
a strained expectation leading onto nothing

quotation
one week we slept like spoons in a drawer
        the next week, the same, but in the other direction

parentheses
the condemned man dreams of his pardon
what I think of when I do not think of you

Vigil

Midnight much worry
in a little room—
strike a match and time
is burning toward you.

Weather

Sounds travel far and wide,
a cow thumps her ribs with her tail,

a rainbow lingers in the morning sky
and a wind comes quickly from the East,

chickens scratch together in the dust,
bees stay close to the hive,

thunder in the morning goes on
into the night, curls droop and evening

grows gray. The cow points her tail
to the East; forests whisper, mountains

roar. The laurel shuts her glossy
door and January fog grows ice.

Mackerel sky, mackerel sky,
not long wet and not long dry.

Sheep gather in a huddle; a circle
glows around the moon, smoke

descends and clouds themselves
pile up like blackest smoke.

A rooster crows in the night,
the cow will scratch her ear,

crows light on the fence, gulls
light on the strand. Fish rise

to the surface, for once eager
to bite. Fog in the hills means

water for the mills and leaves show
their backs to the growing wind.

Mackerel sky, mackerel sky,
not long wet and not long dry.

Ladybugs swarm, crickets speed their
ticks and pigs carry sticks

in their mouths. Crows now
fly in pairs. A rainbow

shines at dusk and wind blows
from the West, wild geese go out

to sea—you see wind before
rain, then it's fair again.

Crows walk about on the ground,
bees stray far on their flight,

thunder in the night is gone
in the day; evening red, morning

gray—and dew on the grass below the cow
who points her tail clearly to the West.

    My love, whenever
you look for the weather,

you look at nothing
more or less than the aftermath

of signs that came before
what is happening

became what is happening.
A mood falls over the present

like a thud or a blackout,
a breeze or a shadow, for

a door has opened up in the heavens
and that door is as likely

to close. We live below
in the cave of will and

stick out a finger from
time to time to test the wind's

direction. Up there it all
depends. You could shake it slowly

through a sieve and still know less
than you knew when you started.

There's no one in that place
with a passing thought for us.

      — VIRGIL, *Georgics,* Book I.351–423

Wings

If you could have wings would you want them?

> I don't know.

I mean, if you could use them to fly, would you want them?

> Yes, if I could fly.

But they would be really big.

> How big?

They might brush against your knees as you walked, or be bigger than some doorways.
And what if you couldn't ever take them off?

> I still would want them.

If you couldn't take them off, even if you were going somewhere,
or going to bed, or eating at a table, or you wanted to pick
someone up, you could never take them off?

> Yes, I would. I would still want them.

Because you could fly?

Yes, because of the flying.

And if they were heavy, or even if no one else had them, and even if
    your children and their children didn't have them?

Yes, I think so.

But you would still have arms and hands and legs, and you could still
    speak, but you had wings, too. You would want the wings, too?

Yes, I would want the wings, too.

And when you were walking around, people would stare at you, and they
    wouldn't necessarily understand that you could fly?

I understand. I understand that they wouldn't understand.

Or if people thought they meant something, something they didn't really
    mean?

I would know what the wings were for.

And if you had them, forever—the forever, I mean, that is your life,
    you would still want them?

Yes, I would want them. I would take them, so long as I could fly.

that I might fly away
    that I might fly away where the ships
        that I might fly away where the ships of pine wood pass between the dark cliffs

X/Cross

Roll back the stone
and find another stone.
No spot, no tracks,
just the trail of
a nail dragged
from a single string.
History starts
with the theft of a cow
and ends with the theft
of a temple.

To You and For You

When you say you are afraid there is something else there, some figure
    by the window, or someone
        coming nearer, a voice in another
           room that isn't
        quite a voice, somehow the difference

between things and persons and the difference between persons and things,

        so given and *irreducible,*

becomes like the clouding of

the past
    and the present at
        the moment when you want to turn
    toward the future

and find yourself leaden
    with hesitation.

        I do not know where the dead are, or if they are. It is as easy
        to say they are with us as to say they are irrevocably gone.

The film you saw, where the boy lives in the midst
    of an afterlife,
        and thinks it is this world, and cannot see
            all the forces that have gathered

            against him, is now in your memory and the memory of others—

        and nowhere else.

He was a boy who never lived, but you are alive,

and your desire to live can overwhelm
        whatever compels you to forget.

            You can risk some harm, run up close
            to the brink,
            and still you won't know what it is you want to know.

No one can look at the sun, and so we look at pictures.

I have seen the soul go out,
            like a breath,
and fill the room
        before it leaves.

            And that was the end of it; there was no second end.

You ask if they have some intent toward us.

        Do they think of us as we think of them? Is it fury
        that drives them,
            or conscience, or regret?

I cannot give you a good explanation, I cannot explain
what good is;

my hope is you will feel it
as a kind of ease.

I've known those who are busy with love, very busy,
and ever vigilant,

those who never take their eyes away, never fall
aslant.

And they, too, are alive,

but they have devoted themselves to fear.

And their fear,
a second end, is like
a form of death.

You understand these are questions you are asking of yourself.

There is no outside
setting them against you.

Your mind made these thoughts
and your mind
will hold you from them.

Zero

Mark a circle and start digging here.

Don't think you are clearing a space

for a foundation, just dig like a mole,

stitching in and out. Tell them your hope

goes down slanting, that everything

inevitable runs toward

the horizontal.

Dig wherever your shadow falls, a green

patch backlit by a blazing

planet—wherever your shadow falls, dig

in the shape of your shadow falling.

III THE ELEMENTS

Favor hates Necessity, hard to endure
— EMPEDOCLES

Wrought from the generation of EARTH

One boot planted, firm as a trunk, the other shoved down on the shovel,
                   shoving with a human weight that barely dents the crust
over the outcrop of flinty veins that plumb through clay and chalk.
                Struck down bluntly over and over, the shovel bounces back,
ringing the facts. Even the dead must wait above ground
                for a hard winter to thaw. Nothing to do but wait, hoping for
the ground to give, hoping the corpse won't wander.
              Freezing up, the bulb cracks, aborting its bloom, and the smaller
half falls away—all things bearing their own teleology,
             all things turning out or not—the husk shrivels back across
the pod and the young mice lie stiff in their nest. Coming to be
                  collapses, radiant as a berry trapped in ice.

Under the dazzle of the white light on the whiteness, only
                the forms remain, a solid geometry slumping at its edges;
you can't tell the difference between a rock and a hard place, or a sled
             and a wheel-barrow sunk into the compost. The tar caddies
steam on every block, buckets of hell-sludge go up single file, plugging
            the gaping roofs, or are passed down to craters where traffic
ruts and wheels are wrenched away. A tomb is pried up, then resealed.
     Skull-duggery, boneyards, dustbins. The endless digging and patching
of the world. A new wound is cut, then healed.
     The dew evaporates from the softening snow; you can see your breath
and know you are breathing and that is enough to make you want to speak
                 in the season of longest nights.

The frail root stirs, a shiver runs down the hinges of the night-crawler, a slight
quiver ruffles across the hunched neck of the wren. One day a breeze arrives,
and her winter wings shake free with each short hop to the seed after next.
It doesn't take a crowbar when the door is open. Mud turns to muck,
the blood begins to thin, the rusted joints are oiled and move again.
The ice breaks and jams the river, sounding like distant guns, while the pitch-
fork goes in and out with ease. What will come back comes back and what
doesn't come back stays, too, somehow nascent or caught within the bramble,
slowly losing its name and form.

The broom sweeps up and wears away, sweeping itself into a stump. Pebble
tags weed and weed tags clod—fatigue of the soiled world, fatigue-dragging
shoe, dragging shoulder and fist, the effort toward consequence, clenched and
released in rhythm. Crops fail or flourish, toys of the weather, and the weather
does not think of us in turn. Spirit who needs a look-out, spirit not in our
image, he drops to the horizon, gathering speed. The absolute form of offering
repeated, the absolute form of earthly repetition, churning and churning
along the furrow.

There by the side of the churning sea, the plowman's bent doubled in the field,
    sees a dark fleck
        —no, white wings—moving toward the sun,
            but does not see his fall, or even dream a man
                could free himself from ground
      and somehow fly.

Work is wrenched from the thick, from the dense, from the places where
resistance is clotted with stones. The rake gets tangled with sticks and vines,
the scythe chips off and leaves a ragged swathe.
Mud muddies the spring and can only be settled by gravity. The sun takes aim
at the nape of the neck, the crown, or right between the eyes.
Spoiled saints listen for miracles while the cooks sift pebbles from the grain.

What is primitive in memory stays buried in memory. Things made of earth
sink deeper into earth and begin to be earth again: a vase blown from sand
and fire; the clay lamp shaped by a hand long dead and water long ago drawn
back into its bed; a spoon thinned into a silver lattice soon to be flecks
of silver again. Deep in the mine, fire flames from the methane
or shines for no reason from the diamond's splinter.

Dust rolls cells and crumbs and lint and binds them loose with hair.
Amber hardens around the spider, the bones melt into the peat.
The soil lies opened to the gaze of the heavens like a memory exposed to light.
Vase, clay lamp, and silver spoon, working loose, come glinting as shards
to the surface.

Went down to the shore where the beach was hard,
                              went right to the edge of the inhabited world,
built a ditch and a castle, a minaret, a draw-bridge,
                              shaping heads and limbs from the sugary sand.
Then fast flung, crashed, a single wave
                              erasing, though every grain of sand remains.

This was the only world, the world where we awakened, where the sky gods
hold one handle of the plow and the gods of the dead hold the other.
The brown gods rose from the mud and the ponds, and crept along the paths
and had no names. And then the gods concealed in gypsum fought against
the fathers, rising up in fury, inconsolable. When the wars of heaven ended,
sky held dominion, dominion over all below.

Deep where the bloodless ghosts assemble, at the still base of the revolving
world, the girl sorted seeds in the lap of her apron, letting each one count
as a month, letting three count as a season, saying six will count as
the darkness and six will count as the light. She sang to herself,
sang the whole day through, knotting rings and necklaces
from coarsest blades of grass. She sang a walking song
and dreamed, her corduroy blanket abandoned to fray and
lint for the birds to weave.

Look for her, lie along the meadow; you can hear the hum
of the stalks and leaves, the full buzz so unlike
a shell's hollow roar. Lie along the field and feel the mineral cold,
bone-chilling deep below the warmth of the loam. Lie in the dead leaves
and do not make a sound and love will cut furrows in the soil of grief.

This was the only world: great scar, worn away by reverence and harm.
Permanence out of which all things that perish rise; permanence in which
each enduring thing will perish. Not the earth surrendered or asunder.
Not the earth itself, but tenderness.

Flown from the generation of WATER

a breath flew across the water, a breath, a thread, of living fire
      that stretched across the surface of the water

and the water moved in time, oblivious, cold as a mirror,
      cold as time itself that mirrors only water,

mirroring water just as water
      coldly mirrors sky—

what I know about the water is written
      in the water, what the water is

is written in the water,
      the weft of water is woven in the water

but the thread of living fire cannot be woven;

everything falls, everything dropping down from where it came,
      a drop oozing from a leaf,

a pear-shaped bead,
      a pendant then pulled up into a sphere,

an egg, a sphere, then pear again, elastic,
       pulled, then a pause

before the pause, the comic
       plop splashed on the stone—

look and listen and you will lose the other,
       the next drop beginning

that will wear this one away, as the drops wear, invisibly,
       the stone back into water—

jug and cup in pieces in the rain,
       kettle in the rain, leaking rain;

take the bucket to the springhouse, go inside the mossy silence,
       dip your arm to the elbow and push against the thickness,

going deeper into water, black into the darkness,
       the source of water waiting there, far beneath the water

and the water black as coal,
       black as any earth-mined thing;

then bring it to the daylight and it will clear
       again, clear in the clear glass, invisible

over hands, a blessing
       falling, a dangling happiness,

blessed nothingness that nothing does not need,

and you will learn to find the source
        of the water, how thirst comes before

the search for the source and searching is a thirst
        that can't be slaked—

you were made from water and you are made of water
        and drawn to it as surely as the forked stick of the dowser

to dissolve like pain or memory,
        to dissolve stirred and drifting,

to disappear into the form of what was always waiting,
        forget what stood as dread or care

there in the distance; rest your head, unthinking
        on the water's lifted palm,

rest your head and all your limbs
        will float like risen weeds—

most beautiful of all things, of all things on the earth,
        is light cast up in motion from

the surface of the water, most beautiful
        of dancing things, the light cast on the bridges, the light cast

on the bow, and on the sleeping faces,
        dancing light from water glancing, wavering, like a voice

where voice is lifted all at once
        out of the heft of words—

what I can write of water melts in the light
      of light on water, the water given, giving, cannot be held

in time; rain driving down against the bridge,
      driving all night without intention,

erasing the hearts and letters scrawled
      across the blocks of stone—declarations of love

and strife, gone in the morning light;
      a white page floats on the surface of the river,

caught in a clutter of branches that flooded
      down from summer storms—

water that carries the memory of mountains into the sea's forgetting,
      water that begins under shadblow and redwood and swirls under

willows in the swollen meadows, washing up a seed or
      carp, bloated on treeless sands,

a message in a bottle stays in the bottle and the bottle
      stays lodged between branches of coral;

distich stitching of oars, catch and slap and ripple,
      S, letter of rivers, sound goes surer the deeper it descends,

far beneath the surface, the invisible wreck,
      while the great logs bob through the skin;

snow on the sea melts into the sea and snow on the river
      melts into the river until the river gathers

into ice below snow, its freezing equation of loss and gain
		and motion hidden from view,

element buoying and resistant, element most flattering to
		error, element deadly to fools and self-deceivers:

lift your head and you will drown—

the water drags you down by the knees, drags you with
		its invisible net, and pulls you under into the minute

where your life unreels its sequence of dreams:
		you were born in the month of water and born from the water's arms

and carried across the ford to the fountain made of nails
		and baptized there in tears where the blue washed over the windows—

country of salt and bitterness, tide of wasted wrack and goads,
		the clothes strewn on the beach like shells, empty as any emptiness;

cause is as distant as snow in the mountains where snow is the cause of all things—

one night in particular,
		night drenched and steaming, a moonless night

on the street of the militia,
		the book of hell lay in the gutter,

the pages oozing, the black print blurred
		back into pulpy weight;

I wrapped it in my coat and carried it to my room
		and laid it, spine up, on the vent

where it steamed like the soggy diaper
        of a long-neglected child,

the pages stiffened apart from each other
        and could not be turned again:

angels and thieves and warriors and liars
        lovers and readers silent in their chambers

stream from the circus of the dead
        parade of blackboards and gowns

silence in the wood and fiercest sun
        glinting from the surface of the sea

long nights beneath the drumming roof
        afternoons pressed by the weight of the water

the clothesline collapsed, the sheets in the mud
        and at morning the dew spread like stardust on the grass—

where is the water of the sopping weight, the water
        shed at the moment of the cry?

where is the water that died into water
        so the water, eddying, would clear away its stain?

breath buried like a treasure under water, breath
        breathing its secret under water,

depth of love and force of strife swept
        by the roiling water, swept

where the warp is woven in the water,

thread of living fire that leaves no scar on water,

thread of living fire that never ends

Notes

[These notes give sources for cited language and allusions when the attribution is not already provided in the text.]

epigraph: *The Theaetetus of Plato,* ed. M. Burnyeat, trans. M. J. Levett. Indianapolis: Hackett, 1990, 197d–198, p. 333. A history of metaphors of the columbarium, the cell, and the book in ancient and medieval memory systems can be found in Mary Carruthers, *The Book of Memory,* Cambridge: Cambridge University Press, 1992, pp. 35–38.

The Elements: For the pre-Socratic view of the elements throughout I have referred to "Empedocles: Fragments and Commentary," ed. and trans. Arthur Fairbanks, *The First Philosophers of Greece.* New York: Scribner, 1898.

"Sung from the generation of AIR*":* The situation of "the memory of happiness" section comes from Dante, *Inferno,* Canto V.

"Drawn from the generation of FIRE*":* For the opening lines, see Friedrich Hölderlin, "Empedokles"; in *Poems and Fragments,* trans. Michael Hamburger, London: Routledge, 1966; for an account of the eruption of Vesuvius, Letter 6.16 in *Letters of Pliny the Younger,* ed. John Boyle, 5th Earl of Orrery, Vol. II, London: printed by James Bettenham for Paul Vaillant, 1752; on shining in Paradise, burning in Hell, burning wood to worship fire, and burning fire to worship wood, Gaston Bachelard, *The Psychoanalysis of Fire,* trans. Alan C. M. Ross, Boston: Beacon, 1964.

georgics: Paraphrases of Virgil's *Georgics* rely on the Loeb edition, ed. H. Rushton Fairclough and revised by G. P. Goold, Cambridge, Mass.: Harvard University Press, 1999, as well as the translations of Cecil Day Lewis, *Virgil's Georgics,* New York: Anchor, 1964.

"Cross/X": Our unrequited affection for dolls is discussed in Rainer Maria Rilke, "Some Reflections on Dolls," in *Selected Works,* Vol. I, trans. G. Craig Houston, London: Hogarth Press, 1954.

"Ellipse": Descriptions of planetary motion are taken from Johannes Kepler, *Epitome of Copernican Astronomy;* trans. C. G. Wallis, New York: Prometheus, 1995 and the

metaphor of magnetic threads from William Gilbert, *De Magnete,* trans. P. Fleury Mottelay, New York: Dover, 1958; "the saint had said" section comes from Augustine of Hippo, *Confessions,* trans. R. S. Pine-Coffin, Book XIII.9, Harmondsworth, Middlesex: Penguin, 1961.

"Forms of Forts": On touching one hand with another, see Maurice Merleau-Ponty, *Phenomenology of Perception,* London: Routledge, 1989, p. 315.

"Kingfisher Carol": The epigraph comes from the *Standard Dictionary of Folklore, Mythology, and Legend,* ed. Maria Leach, New York: Funk and Wagnalls, 1949; "the darkness knows it not," John 1:5.

"Now in the minute": "Now goþ sonne vnder wod," (Anonymous), *English Lyrics of the XIIIth Century,* Vol. I, ed. Carleton Brown; John Donne, Oxford: Oxford University Press, 1932; John Donne, "The Sunne Rising," *The Complete English Poems,* London: Penguin, 1976.

"O": Peleus's grieving is drawn from Euripides, *Andromache,* 1200, trans. Susan Stewart and Wesley Smith, New York: Oxford University Press, 2002; Hecuba's barking is from Ovid, *Metamorphoses,* Book XIII, trans. Mary Innes, London: Penguin, 1955 and Dante, *Inferno,* Canto XXX.

"Pear": "the given world is infinite," Immanuel Kant, *Critique of Pure Reason,* trans. Paul Guyer and Allen Wood, Cambridge: Cambridge University Press, 1998.

"The History of Quiver": Oxford English Dictionary

"Rewind": Quoted language is from Søren Kierkegaard, *The Seducer's Diary,* trans. Hong and Hong, Princeton, N.J.: Princeton University Press, 1987.

"The Seasons": The shepherd's death is from James Thomson, "Summer," *The Seasons,* Philadelphia: Prichard and Hall, 1788.

"These Trees in Particular": The planetree is from Plato, *Phaedrus,* trans. Alexander Nehamas and Paul Woodruff, Indianapolis: Hacket, 1995.

"Lost Rules of Usage": "strained expectation leading onto nothing," Immanuel Kant, *Critique of the Power of Judgment,* 5:333, trans. Paul Guyer and Eric Matthews, Cambridge: Cambridge University Press, 2000.

"Wings": Euripides, *Andromache,* 862–65.

"To You and For You": On the sun and narrating pictures, Ludwig Wittgenstein, *The Brown Book,* pp. 51–55, *The Blue and Brown Books,* London: Harper, 1958.